Praying Children in the Home

by
Jane Keiller
Wife, mother and non-stipendiary Deacon at St. Barnabas Church, Cambridge

GROVE BOOKS LIMITED
Bramcote Nottingham NG9 3DS

CONTENTS

THE COVER PICTURE

is by Hannah Higginson

ACKNOWLEDGEMENTS

Many people have contributed to this booklet by their williness to share from their own personal and family experiences; to each I offer my heartfelt thanks. The Higginson family and the Seddon family have made very special contributions by sharing their experiences of several years of growing Christian families. I would also like to thank Amiel Osmaston, Lawrence and Di Osborn as well as Felicity Higginson and Debbie Seddon for their constructive help and encouragement, to pay tribute to Sally Bott for her patience and typing, and to Andrew as always.

First Impression August 1992

ISSN 0262-799X
ISBN 1 85174 217 4

INTRODUCTION

It was Shrove Tuesday. I had decided against pancakes for tea. The previous year we had invited friends and had a party, but none of the children like pancakes. As we walked home from school, Sarah, aged 4½, said 'Please Mummy, may we have pancakes? We made them at school and I love them.'

We arrived home and began measuring out the flour. 'Quick, Mummy, look what James is doing!' I groaned as I watched the salt pouring in vast quantities on top of the flour.

Cooking with small children makes me so bad-tempered!

The pancakes finally made, there followed a conversation about Shrove Tuesday, Ash Wednesday, Jesus in the desert and Lent. 'What do people do on Ash Wednesday?' asked Sarah. I told her what friends of ours did last year as their family of six sat around the tea table. She listened attentively and then said with great finality, 'I don't like saying "sorry" '!

That was the end of a great start to Lent—for this year at least.

We are not an unusually spiritual family! As Christian parents, however, we do long to share our faith with our three young children. We have prayed for them since before they were born and are filled with wonder as they grow and develop their individual personalities. There will come a time when they will need to choose for themselves whether or not to follow Jesus Christ. In the meantime our desire is to show them as much as we can of the love of their Heavenly Father, to teach them his Word, to pray for them and with them and to have as much fun as possible in the process.

From 1988 to 1990 we lived in Muscat, Oman, and during that time we enjoyed the friendship of a British Christian family working with an international company. They knew that it would be most likely that their children would be at school in England whilst the parents continued to live and work overseas. The parents were aware that the length of time the children would be living continuously at home with them was limited, but they haven't allowed the eleventh birthday of their eldest child to creep up on them unawares. They have prayed and planned and discussed the things that they hope they will have taught their children by the time each comes to fly off to boarding school.

I was challenged by their thinking—our circumstances are different, but the underlying truth is the same: the length of time our children are living with us, cared for and nurtured by us is limited. What do we hope to teach them? What gifts and strengths should we encourage? How can we respond to God's call to us to raise our children in a manner pleasing to him? How can we teach our children the ways they should go so that when they are grown they won't depart from them?

The needs of families with teenagers deserve a booklet of their own. This one is for the parents of children of twelve years and under. I hope it may prove to be a catalyst for all kinds of creativity in the ways we provide for the spiritual growth of our families.

1. BACKGROUND

In her book, *Child of the Covenant*, Michele Guinness writes, 'Christians uphold family life as the key to a well-ordered society. Jews uphold family life as the key to the survival of Judaism. That is the secret of its success.'[1] Without wanting to idealize family life or glorify the home, I am convinced that Michele Guinness is right, and that both are greatly under-used when it comes to the Christian nurture of our children.

A home has to be positively dangerous to a child before removal is seen to be a better option. Home, for all its imperfect inhabitants, holds a unique position in the growth and development of a child; whether it's a castle or a caravan, it is here that a child learns about who he is, about where she belongs. It is here that learning takes place on so many different levels.

Much of Jesus' teaching and ministry takes place in homes. He enters individual homes in order to heal (Peter's mother-in-law Matt. 8.14; Jairus' daughter. Matt. 9.23). He makes conscious decisions to visit homes which amaze onlookers and transform the occupants (Matthew/ Levi the tax collector, Matt. 9.10; Zaccheus, Luke 19.5-9)

The intimate atmosphere of dinner in someone's home not only provides the context for individual conversion, as in the case of Matthew and Zacchaeus, but also allows for personal expressions of love which trigger some of Jesus' more difficult teaching, as, for example, the issue of the apparent waste of perfume poured over Jesus' feet during dinner (Luke 7.36; John 12), and his teaching to Mary and Martha (Luke 10). It is of course in the context of a shared meal that Jesus teaches his disciples the meaning of his death. The fact that we have formalized this into the communion service means that we often fail to make the connexion with the value of teaching round the table with family and friends gathered together in this most basic form of human intimacy.

The Old Testament makes it clear that parents have a special calling to teach and train their children in the ways of God.
> 'Impress them [the commandments] on your children, talk about them when you sit at home and when you walk along the road, when you lie down and when you get up.' (Deuteronomy 6.7).

This presupposes that talking to our children about God and his laws should be a normal, regular occurrence. The Jews were to do this wherever they were, day or night. A child growing up in a Jewish home learns about his heritage through the special festivals of the Jewish year, through the family *sader* meal on a Friday night, and the keeping of the Sabbath. God is at home, not just in the synagogue.

This booklet is offered to all parents who want their homes to be a place where their children will learn to know and love God, where children will grow up knowing where they belong, where following Christ is exciting, challenging and fun.

[1] Michele Guinness, *Child of the Covenant* (Hodder and Stoughton, London, 1985), p.149.

2. PARENTS PRAYING

The desire to raise children who pray has to begin with the parents' prayer life. We all know that example is the most powerful teaching force, and children who see and hear their Mums and Dads speaking with and listening to their Heavenly Father learn more about prayer than any amount of formal teaching on prayer can ever give them. And yet it is notoriously difficult for the parents of small children to establish, or even continues in a regular pattern of prayer.

Most adult Christians who have learnt to appreciate the benefits of a period of quiet with God at the beginning of the day, find the arrival of small children devastating to their spiritual lives. To wake up before an under-five can be quite difficult for the average parent, to succeed and then to be joined by that child, who has woken to the sounds of your footsteps is not usually conducive to prayer. I have read of women who had quiet times between 2 a.m. and 3 a.m., they are made of tougher stuff than I am. So what do the rest of us do?

If we see our families as a gift from God then we can't at the same time behave as if they are a trap to draw us away from him. If I hold onto impossible ideals the result will be guilt, frustration and spiritual alienation. The alternative, for me, has been to put together a patchwork prayer life, lots of pieces which together provide the fabric of my Godward journey. Sometimes the pieces seem very small, but looking back I see colour and pattern and, most important of all, the hand of God in our lives.

Foundational to all my 'pieces of prayer' has been the discovery that God speaks to me through my children and through the experience of being a parent. So often the Bible describes God's work with humankind through the images of parenthood, both father and mother, and, if I will allow myself the privilege, there are new insights for me to grasp by using my own experiences as a parent to help me understand the Word of God more deeply. From the moment I first held my daughter Sarah in my arms I learnt something more of the desperate pain felt by God in the face of his wayward children. The thought of bearing children, loving them, nurturing them and for them to turn and rebel against us is too terrible to contemplate. Yet all the images of God as conceiving, bearing, delivering children are there in Scripture and so often the children are deaf to the parent, unresponsive, going their own way.[1] Images are, of course, only images. God is neither man nor woman; he is infinitely greater. Yet all of us faced with the life-changing circumstances which parenthood brings need to consider what our image of God is. We all need the assurance that 'He tends his flock like a shepherd: he gathers the lambs in his arms and carries them close to his heat; he gently leads those that have young' (Isaiah 40.11).

[1] Examples of mother images: Psalm 131.2; Isaiah 42.14; Isaiah 45.10-11; Isaiah 49.15; Isaiah 66.7-13; Job 38.28-29; Matthew 23.37/Luke 13.34 Examples of father images. Isaiah 63.16; Hosea 11.1-4; Matthew 6.9; Matthew 7.11; Luke 15.11-31; John 1.12; Romans 8.15.

Having talked with many parents about their personal prayer life, I find that flexibility seems to be the key to 'success'. Children change so rapidly in the early years and what had seemed an interminable phase may suddenly be over. It may once again be possible to be quiet for half an hour early in the morning, or during Sesame Street or while a child is asleep. There may on the other hand, be times when it is appropriate to abandon all attempts at a longer time of prayer and to rely solely on shorter prayers scattered throughout the day. The following are ideas which have been found helpful by those who have shared with me some of their secrets of praying as parents.

1. Moment Prayers

I suppose these are more traditionally known as arrow prayers, but, as I tend to associate arrow prayers with crises, then I would like to make a differentiation. Moment prayers have meant for me consciously taking opportunities to pray whilst undertaking the countless small, and often mindless, tasks of mothering. Many parents seem to pray for their children the last time they look at them before going to bed. However, there are countless other times throughout a day when, if we choose, we can 'pray for a moment'; preparing food, ironing, tidying up, settling children to sleep and so on. Everyday images of feeding and clothing are plentiful in the New Testament and they can easily be used to focus short prayers for the family.[1]

A friend who went on a retreat recently was encouraged to take a minute at intervals throughout the day to focus on her relationship with God. She was recommended to stand firmly wherever she was and repeat several times 'I am rooted in the love of God'. Obviously any thought focussing on a promise of God would be equally appropriate. Someone who finds such short meditation helpful might do well to spend a few minutes at the beginning of a week to choose a verse or a phrase which can then punctuate the following days.

Prayer Chains

The church women's group to which I belong operates a prayer chain, which has been a great source of help and encouragement. There are, in fact, three chains:
a) at 9 a.m.
b) at 1 p.m.
c) at 7 p.m.
The different times allow for most people to work round the vagaries of fetching and carrying children and other out-of-home employment or commitments. The chain requires a link person to whom a request can be telephoned, who will provide the list of names and phone numbers so that one can phone down the list until someone replies. There needs to be a basic set of guidelines for each member which encourages them
a) to keep a notebook and pencil handy to write down prayers, so that details are passed on correctly.
b) to pass on the information without gossip.
c) to ring the next person on the chain immediately and then to stop and pray before carrying on with whatever else one was doing.

[1] E.g. Matthew 6.25; John 6.57,58; 1 Peter 2.2,3; Ephesians 6.11; Isaiah 61.10; Colossians 3.12; Romans 13.14.

The value of these prayers has been enormous. They provide a resource for the church leadership so that PCCs and other important decision-making times are prayed for. They also provide prayer support for those feeling especially isolated, for example when children are ill or spouses away or indeed totally absent.

3. Praying with others
Not every parent has a spouse to pray with and even those who do often find that there is great value in finding someone else to pray with specifically for their homes and families. If there are small children present this will probably be noisy and frequently interrupted, but the children get used to seeing their parents pray and it means that details of life which can often seem so trivial can still be prayed for, wisdom sought and answers found.

My husband, Andrew, and I pray together last thing at night, but I have to confess that I frequently fall asleep before we've finished. This has left me feeling bad about the way we, as parents, pray for our children, and so we have tried to fix in the diary an evening on a monthly basis which we set aside to think specifically about each child, to discuss needs, to make plans of specific ways in which we can help and to seek God's wisdom about how we can best parent each child. I have other friends who do this weekly. The timing is not so important as the fact that we do it. Even an annual review would mean that we are at least planning and praying constructively rather than waiting to respond to whatever crisis next appears in the life of each child.

Parenting can bring great joy, but it is fraught with pitfalls too. Those of us blessed with a believing spouse should consider those within the church family who struggle alone. It is not always easy to offer to pray with someone, especially if we don't know them well, but the worst that can happen is that they'll say 'No, thank you'!

4. Using the Bible to pray for our children
Quinn Sherrer in her book *How to Pray for Your Children*[1] has encouraged me to hunt out biblical promises and prayers to pray specifically for my children. This has had many benefits:
a)   It is a lovely way to pray for babies who frequently don't have needs in such an obvious way as older children.

b)   It is a way of bringing praise and worship into our prayers for our children.

c)   It is a way of keeping us dipping into our Bibles.

Reflect on the examples on the next page.

[1] Quinn Sherrer, *How to Pray for Your Children* (Kingsway Publications, Eastbourne, 1990) p.24ff.

Examples:

—Teach John your ways so he may know you and continue to find favour with you. (Exodus 33.13)

—Show Emily your ways, O Lord, teach her your paths; guide her in your truth and teach her, for you are God her Saviour. May her hope be in you all day long. (Psalm 25.4,5)

—Whether Rebecca turns to the right or the left, may her ears hear a voice behind her, saying, 'This is the way, walk in it.' (Isaiah 30.21)

—Lord, I thank you that you have plans for Adam, plans to prosper him and not to harm him, plans to give him a hope and a future. I pray that he will not walk in the counsel of the wicked, or stand in the way of sinners, or sit in the seat of mockers. But that his delight will be in the love of the Lord, and that he will meditate on it day and night. (Jeremiah 29.11, Psalm 1.1,2)

—Father, give Tom the Spirit of wisdom and revelation, so that he may know you better. (Ephesians 1.17)

A small notebook for each child or a card index can be helpful and will produce a spiritual treasure trove over the years.

3. TEACHING OUR CHILDREN TO PRAY

'Train a child in the way he should go, and when he is old he will not turn from it.' (Proverbs 22.6).

Perhaps this Proverb sounds too glib in this secular day and age where many of us have friends agonizing with rebellious teenagers; and yet no-one seems to doubt the fact that the early years are of vital importance in the development of each individual. They are the years when we learn the most with the greatest facility. Future patterns of relationships, emotional maturity and intellectual growth, all have their foundations laid in the 0-7 years. When an American friend of mine told me that all the scripture verses that come most easily to her mind were taught to her by her mother before she was 10 years old, it brought home to me afresh the opportunity and the responsibility of these early years. Having talked with people who were brought up in a home where they were taught to pray and read the bible, as well as those who came to know Christ later in their life, I am convinced that to grow up in the context of a loving Christian home is a priceless gift; even those who rebel acknowledge that they learned things about decision-making, about knowing right from wrong, about respect and individual worth for which they will always be grateful.

That we should teach our children to pray is something most Christian parents acknowledge. How we go about it often raises many questions. How do we set patterns without them degenerating into duty and superstition? If our children are hearing bible stories from before they are two, how do we prevent them from becoming so familiar that they are deaf to their message in later life? How do we help them to hear God's voice and love his Word?

There can be no system which is right for every family. We are all different and what one family enjoys may be awkward and embarrassing to another. Families where only one parent is a Christian will have different things to work out and the Christian parent will need to consult with the unbelieving partner so that conflict doesn't occur.

Making the most of opportunities

Children have no problems talking about God. If they go to church, if they have Bible stories read to them then they will have myriads of questions about what he looks like, where he lives, why we die, why he made things and how. Often questions like these come at bedtime, possibly because many parents pray with their children before they sleep, but probably because children always seem to want to prolong the time before the parent leaves the room—questions about life, the universe and everything come in very handy! Any question about God and the big issues of life is an opportunity to teach our children spiritual truth. It doesn't need to be a 'heavy session'. A reply may take only a moment but the way we respond may tell them more than what we actually say. I shall always be grateful that my parents talked and discussed with me. From an early age I knew that they were interested in what I thought and that my opinion was valued. It was a significant factor in the development of my own self-worth as well as my understanding of the world. If we reply readily to our children it makes talking about God something 'we do' as a family, something that is a pleasure, something that isn't awkward or embarrassing, and if we do it when the children are four, six, eight then we're more likely to be doing it when they are fourteen, sixteen, eighteen.

Our children enjoy listening to tapes especially in the car, and Christian praise tapes are some of their favourites. Ishmael has made a huge contribution to children's worship and in an enjoyable and effortless manner the whole family is learning scripture because we are learning his songs; verse after verse, often with the reference included, set to music which is easily accessible and great fun. Some of these tapes are too expensive for frequent purchase, but we try to buy one before our summer holiday. It's good to have something new to listen to and the songs become associated with all kinds of good and happy memories. A major festival or an anniversary, perhaps after a baptism would be an equally appropriate time.

Most children enjoy singing. The cry of 'Mummy, listen to the song I've made up' is a familiar one. We are *not* a musical family and usually these 'songs' are impossible to recall after the first singing. Occasionally however something is said or sung which, with a little bit of help, can become part of a family repertoire. We had an example recently when Sarah sang a somewhat lengthier version of 'Oh God, thank you for all the lovely things you've given me today' with a little pruning, by adding 'Oh God' three times at the beginning and 'Thank you, Lord' at the end. We set it to Frere Jaques and instantly had an extremely useful highly adaptable family praise song. Families where a parent plays a musical instrument have a wonderful resource; singing together not only means that children are praising, and enjoying praising God, but memories are created which will last a lifetime. Nothing is being said explicitly, but vital truth is learnt and experienced.

Different Kinds of Prayer

For some people the idea of praying within the home can have claustrophobic connotations. The thought of organizing daily family prayers with wriggly toddlers and only half-interested children can seem too off-putting to contemplate. In many families the reality can never match up to some idealised view of parents and children sitting down together to pray and read the Bible. Then sadly, because that isn't an option, nothing else in the way of praying together is attempted either.

For me the verse in Deuteronomy about teaching our children the ways of God when we sit at home and when we walk along the road, when we lie down and when we get up (Deuteronomy 6.7) is helpful because it indicates a process, part of the journey of life. There will be times in all our families when bad things happen, when people we love are sick or dying, when relationships we value are broken, when we are hurt and downhearted. The image of a journey is a valuable one, it means that such times can be passed through; they don't have to threaten to destroy all that we hold dear. A further advantage of the journey image is that it is something parents and children can do together with friends and members of the extended family.

10

In the General Synod's report, *Children in the Way*[1], the image of pilgrimage is used to describe the Church. The authors make the point that the image of the spiritual journey helps us to understand that the communication isn't all from adult to child, sometimes the children will lead. Indeed Jesus himself made it clear that unless we become like little children we will not enter the Kingdom of Heaven. In countless ways children will inspire, challenge, point us Godward. It is important for our children to realize that learning to pray isn't like learning to ride a bicycle. It is something we will spend a life time learning, but there are some things we can do which will help us along the way.

1. Short Prayers

There are many occasions during a day when a short prayer may be appropriate—accidents, anxieties and special joys can all make prayer seem more 'real' to a young child. By the end of the day small children are often very tired and asking them what they would like to pray for can result in fooling around. They simply don't remember the details of the day or by bedtime they can't be bothered. An arrow prayer on the way to school, after a birthday party, before a trip to the doctor's can all help the growing child to learn that God is involved with the details of their life.

Grace before meals is a similar opportunity. The shorter and simpler such prayers are, the more likely the children will be prepared to say grace themselves. Our family enjoys singing grace. We have learned some from friends and passed ours on to others, but I am aware that our children are all small and the age spread is not great. In families where there is a larger gap between siblings, and where older ones express embarrassment when they have friends invited for tea, it is worth considering whether one should carry on regardless or pander to sensibilities. One friend told me how, in their household, to cope with just such a situation a table-cloth was used. The family didn't normally use a table-cloth, but if there was one on the table all the family knew there would be no grace.

2. Bedtime Prayers and Bible Reading

Most children seem to find great security in a ritual at bedtime. My brother had a long litany which he had to go through every night with our mother. He said something and she replied. Occasionally it was added to and woe to my mother if she forgot her lines! Bedtime is an obvious time to read the Bible and pray with our children. If we usually read to them, then it is not difficult to make one or two of these stories Bible stories. I know one family where ordinary stories are read downstairs, but the Bible story is reserved for bed. This is an attempt to distinguish between the two 'types' of story. Our Sarah has come up with her own way of identifying what is 'real' and what isn't. She talks of Storybookland and The Real World. Goblins, fairies, monsters, talking animals, etc. belong to Storybookland. People can live here too, but these stories aren't 'real'. the Bible belongs to The Real World but a long time ago. As children grow older other categories need to be included, traditional myths and legends for example or some of the stories of the saints. Children learn that some of these are 'true on the inside' if not on the outside[2] and truth can be learnt even if the details are dubious.

[1] *Children in the Way: New Directions for the Church's Children* (National Society, Church House Publishing, London, 1988)
[2] See Gertrud Mueller Nelson, *To Dance with God* (Paulist Press, New York, 1986) p.76.

Some kind of Bible reading aid can be appropriate, even from a young age. The resource section inside the front cover includes suggestions for notes for different ages.

Some children have no problem thinking of endless people and things to pray for, others are as likely to say 'Thank you God for squashed tomatoes'! So how do we help our sometimes reluctant or distracted prayers? A prayer book or card index may help. These require a certain amount of parental organization but they add variety and interest and minimize the opportunity for mucking about! Photos of friends and family can be stuck into pages or onto cards, other non-photogenic prayers can be written down or even drawn. These can then be put into groups—family, friends, church, world needs, etc. Other sections for praise, saying sorry and thank you can also be added. At prayer time the child can choose one or two cards from each section or pick them out if they are being rotated.

Teaching children set prayers can also be enjoyable and give them a great sense of achievement. The Lord's Prayer may seem daunting, but most children are used to learning by heart and don't find it particularly difficult. The Lord's Prayer can be divided into manageable chunks and learnt over a period of weeks.

3. Learning Bible Verses
The same is, of course, true of Bible verses. Many parents however, like the idea of teaching their children Bible verses, but don't really know where to start. How do we work out a retrieval system so that in later years they can recall what they have learnt? The following is an account of one mother's experience of teaching Bible verses to her children. They are a family with three children and when they began the eldest was eight and the youngest three. A Bible learning night has now been established for four years and, according to the children, there would be a riot if it were abandoned. Passages which have been memorized include several psalms, the whole of Ephesians 6 and verses held together by a common theme. Each passage or group of verses is learned over a period of several weeks. They first read the verses, then they begin to memorize the first section. After this they discuss it together, what the passage means and how it relates to their lives, and they memorize the section again. Each child has a quality hard-back book with plain pages in it. The mother lightly writes the section/verse being learned in pencil on one page. The children then go over it, embellishing and decorating the letters and borders and illustrating the meaning on the opposite page where appropriate. After this they pray together about what the verse means to them.

4. Family Prayers
I have a number of friends, including my husband, who come from families where there were daily family prayers, either at breakfast time or in the evening. As I have mentioned before, for some the thought of such an enterprise conjures up a level of organization which appears to be constantly out of reach. However, for many parents a simple reading from a Bible most appropriate to the ages of the children involved, and a few minutes praying together can provide an excellent framework for teaching

children from a very young age how to pray. It can be a time when a missionary is especially prayed for, or an 'adopted' child from overseas, or some world issue that is currently in the news. I know of one family who allow their three-year-old to pray first and then if he wants to he is free to leave while the parents pray for the events of the day. He usually stays and listens quietly. Perhaps the most important ingredient in making family prayers a success is flexibility. What is appropriate with pre-school children may become an unbearable burden when deadlines become tight.

Another option would be to forge out family together time on a weekly basis. Pressures from work, extra school activities, and uniformed organisations not to mention church meetings can all keep the individual family members apart and there is great value in corporate activity, learning and prayer.

Some families choose an evening when they have all eaten together and then move into some joint activity involving games, crafts, acting, even an outing, a few minutes of sharing and teaching and some prayer. Part of a Sunday afternoon can also be used in this way. The following section, 'Family Specials for the Church's Year' includes a number of ideas for family time at festivals. More ideas for use on a weekly basis can be found in *Together at Home* by Dean and Grace Merrill.[1] Such times can help our children reach out to others, make things for a lonely neighbour, visit someone who is sick. One family used this time to pray for eight members of a Russian village imprisoned for their faith. They wrote to their families, sent cards to the prisoners and after several months they saw them all released, one after another. It has been a special time of learning to care for others and of the power of prayer.

1 Dean and Grace Merrill, *Together at Home* (Kingsway Publications, Eastbourne, 1990).

4. FAMILY SPECIALS FOR THE CHURCH'S YEAR

One Easter when I was about three years old I went into the garden and dug a hole which I then carefully lined with grass and leaves. Fortunately my mother heard about my activities and from that year on making the Easter nest was my own little tradition. The first thing I did on Easter morning was to race into the garden to find the eggs for my brother and myself which would then be boiled for breakfast. We always claimed they tasted nicer than ordinary eggs; my mother told me years later that it took her ages to scrub off the little lion that used to be stamped on the shells! One year she tried to amuse me with a joke: The eggs were duly handed over for boiling, but when I sat down to breakfast and cracked the top of the shell it wasn't what I was expecting at all, it was full of solid chocolate. I burst into tears and although it must have happened over thirty years ago, the occasion is still vivid in my memory.

My reaction was perhaps due to being a rather highly-strung little girl, but I think also it might have something to do with expectations, with the security that comes from knowing that some things happen every year, with family traditions and rituals. Children very quickly learn what 'we' do and though they like surprises and treats, they also like the security of something which is special (because it doesn't happen often) but familiar (because it happened last year).

In her excellent book *To Dance with God*, Gertrud Mueller Nelson writes:
> 'There is something very special about the yearly repetition of a smell or flavour. In a world that changes faster and faster, where little remains the same from year to year, it is satisfying and comforting to be able to rely on some things. The return of smells and flavours seems to validate the season at hand and remind us of past feasts'.[1]

Smells and flavours obviously mean mealtime celebrations, but other traditions that don't involve eating can also give enormous pleasure, and provide the setting for teaching religious truths.

I am well aware that I am writing as a 'full-time' mother. For many families where both parents are in paid employment some of the following could become a burden. The idea behind this section has not been to make a long list of suggestions suitable for everyone, but rather activities which might be fun. It is up to the parents to decide how much they will attempt with their family. It is usually up to the children to decide what then becomes tradition; they won't forget something they really enjoyed.

It doesn't need to be expensive to celebrate throughout the Christian year, but I have found it worthwhile to make small investments in items which help to make certain things special. A collection of cake decorations, for example, can be very useful. Books of ideas can also be helpful and there is a list of suggestions inside the front cover. Specialist kitchen shops, good stationers and Christian bookshops can all provide useful items which will prove their value over the years.

[1] Gertrud Mueller Nelson, *op. cit.*, p.158.

It is worth warning at the outset that there is a fundamental problem with a large number of traditions associated with the Christian year and that has to do with when they should be started. Many activities are enormous fun for children between the ages of six and twelve, but it is no good waiting for the youngest to be of an age for full participation before we start. Of course that's not to say that new ideas can't be introduced as the years go by, but the fact of celebrating needs to be established fairly early on. This will frequently involve attempting activities which have great potential for being completely wrecked by young participants—salt in the pancakes, fingers in the icing, fights over who will do what and when; it can sometimes be overwhelmingly tempting to give up. A very simple illustration may help us to persevere. Decorating the Christmas tree is a tradition which is likely to evoke memories for all those reading this booklet. Most of us will have moved from total non-participation to being given the entire job to do with the help of siblings. In the meantime there will have been countless broken baubles, fallings off chairs, eatings of sweets that should have been left for later, but for the sake of wonderful memories these are a small price to pay. There are bound to be disastrous afternoons that were meant to be treats, times when Christian virtues of peace and goodwill seem distinctly lacking, but the human mind is wonderfully selective and I believe that anything we can do to help build up a bank of happy memories, teaching our children the ways of God, is very well worth doing.

1. Advent
In today's secular society Christmas seems to start ever earlier. We may be sickened by tinsel and piped dreamings of a white Christmas in October, but Christian parents need to work hard in order to combat the pleas for Christmas trees in November. The season of Advent provides us with an ideal opportunity for the family to get ready for Christmas without grasping that season's delights too early. Advent, meaning 'coming', is traditionally a season of preparation and penitence. When it arrives we are left with four weeks until Christmas and quite long enough, if we use it creatively, to make ready without the children getting too excited too soon.

Over the years, we have collected a number of Christian books which are kept special by being put away at the end of January and brought out again at the beginning of Advent. It is worth taking the time to browse in the children's section of a good Christian bookshop at the beginning of the autumn to see what is available and perhaps purchase something new to add to the enjoyment of this year's Advent preparation. If the church you attend runs a bookstall try to encourage the organizer to spend a week focusing on seasonal children's books. Last year our church women's group spent a session discussing Advent and Christmas traditions and had available on sale or return a large selection of books and Advent calendars. It proved a good opportunity to ask others what their families enjoy and what wasn't worth the expense! *Here comes Christmas*[1] is a useful little book to help younger children enjoy Advent.

[1] Jenny Gubb *Here comes Christmas* (The National Society/Church House Publishing, London 1990).

Wreaths and Candles

The tradition of Advent candles can turn the most ordinary Sunday tea into an occasion. When it is dark outside by four o'clock, there is something wonderfully exciting about gathering round a candle-lit tea table. Advent candles which are intended to be burnt a little each day are widely available, but many families also enjoy making an Advent wreath with four candles, one for each Sunday in Advent, and these can of course be burnt for a much longer period. There are a number of explanations for the symbols behind each candle and over several years different alternatives can be focused on. Here are some suggestions for starters:

a) 1—Promise
   2—Light
   3—Love
   4—Hope
b) 1—God's gift to us in sending Jesus
   2—Being content with our gifts
   3—Giving to the needy or ill
   4—Jesus' ultimate gift to us, eternal life.[1]

The Wreath

It is possible to buy wrought-iron candle holders in the shape of a wreath. These are expensive, but over a lifetime of family advents are probably worth purchasing. They have the advantage of holding the candles securely and can easily be decorated with evergreens and red ribbon.

We use a circular flower vase which when filled with oasis provides a reasonably firm basis for the candles. It is also possible to keep it watered so the foliage doesn't wither. Another possibility is to take a good-sized bowl filled with damp earth. The candles can then be sunk into it and the rest of the bowl decorated with greenery and ribbon.

The circle is a symbol of eternity, the fact that God goes on for ever. The evergreens stand for eternal life: we were saved to live with God for ever. The candles remind us of Jesus, the Light of the World.

A number of books provide ways of making a wreath using wire, including Joanna Bogle, *A Book of Feasts and Seasons*[2] and Tony Castle, *Let's Celebrate*[3]. Using the wreath to light the Sunday teas of Advent can provide an excellent introduction to family together time.

Calendars

Advent calendars originated in Germany about a hundred years ago, and are commonplace amongst today's children. However, it is worth trying to find one which focuses on the Christmas story and not on some glittery North Pole scene. There are calendars available which gradually tell the story, some have Bible verses printed inside the doors, others portray a Bethlehem scene and slowly the picture changes as the events unfold.

[1] Dean and Grace Merrill, *op. cit.* p.36.
[2] Joanna Bogle, *A Book of Feasts and Seasons* (Fowler Wright Books, Leominster, 1988).
[3] Tony Castle, *Let's Celebrate* (Hodder & Stoughton, London, 1984).

In her book, *Feasting for Festivals*[1], Jan Wilson suggests making an advent calendar using 24 small matchboxes stuck together and covered with pretty wrapping paper to make a little chest of drawers. Each 'drawer' has a number on it and a little something popped inside and/or a verse of scripture and the children can take turns to open it. This would be fun for an older child to make for younger siblings and as children grow older they may enjoy collecting items to go in the boxes.

Another idea would be to make an advent calendar, but just with five doors, one for each Sunday in Advent and one for Christmas Day. Old Christmas cards provide a useful source of pictures to place behind the flaps.

Using 6 December
When we lived in Muscat, we first discovered Sinter Klaas through the Dutch community there. Sinter Klaas is the affectionate name that Dutch children have for St. Nicholas, and on the evening of 5 December they traditionally put out their shoes for the goodies that Sinter Klaas brings. I find him very helpful. I still remember the sense of being let down when I first discovered the truth about Father Christmas; and lurking somewhere in the back of my mind, as the children have grown older, has been the fear that as they grow to understand that Father Christmas isn't real, so they will assume that Jesus isn't either. Sinter Klaas, our Santa Claus, St. Nicholas, can step into the breach. Although it is difficult to discern fact from legend he was a real man, a bishop of Myra on the south coast of Turkey, who lived in the fourth century. There are many stories told of his kindness, but one tells of how he enabled three poor sisters to be married by providing their dowries—three bags of gold. He is believed to have died on 6 December 326 AD.

On 5 December we talk about Saint Nicholas and the kind things he did and the children put their slippers very carefully beside their bed. In the morning they are filled with chocolate money. They know perfectly well that St. Nicholas didn't arrive in person during the night, but they are excited nonetheless by the chocolate and they are learning in a gentle way that St. Nicholas is where our Father Christmas came from. Hopefully that glorious feeling of a full stocking on the end of the bed will never be spoilt, but neither will they be in danger of putting Jesus in the same category as Father Christmas. *A Book of Feasts and Seasons* and *Feasting for Festivals* both contain recipes suitable for celebrating the festival of St. Nicholas.

2. Christmas
Ever since Christmas 1223, when Francis of Assisi brought together the inhabitants of the Italian town of Greccio with an ox and an ass and a manger, Christian people have used the crib scene to help them appreciate the simplicity, poverty and humility of the coming of the Christ child. A beautifully carved crib is lovely to have, but they are usually expensive to buy. There are, however, many alternatives.

Some families enjoy following Francis' lead and dress everybody up in tea towels and dressing gowns. This can be huge fun, especially if visiting

[1] Jan Wilson, *Feasting for Festivals* (Lion, Oxford, 1990) p.14.

family and friends are prepared to join in. The host family needs to work out in advance who is going to be what and have some idea of 'costumes'. This can begin as little more than a simple tableau when children are very small and can become more elaborate as they grow older. Different rooms in the house can be used. The shepherds starting in one room, the kitchen perhaps, the stable could be in the main living area, the wise men could set off from upstairs or outside if you live in a flat. If you are very keen to keep Epiphany for the wise men then you will need to make sure they don't 'arrive' in the stable on Christmas Eve; they will need to take off their crowns and become 'audience' in the living room, and they can resume their duties on 6 January!

It is possible to find crib figures very reasonably priced. I recently saw a twelve-piece set available at £2.99.[1] It would not be difficult to make a stable using wood or stiff cardboard and a scene can then be built up. Several years ago now I made a crib using only cardboard and scraps of fabric. It is simple but the children love it. The kings always start a long way away and make their slow progression round the room—Gertrud Mueller Nelson has a delightful idea of encouraging the children to collect straw for the crib:

'For every good deed—a sacrifice, a brave waiting, a job well done—a straw is placed in the manger as graphic sign of growth and preparation for the Christ Child we await.'[2]

She also provides a suggestion box for when 'being good' is too abstract. A tissue box makes an ideal container and can be decorated with Advent symbols. Inside are suggestions colour-coded for each child: Set the table; share a toy kindly; read a story to your brother; tidy your bedroom; brush the dog; wash the bath . . .

This all adds to a sense of preparation before Christmas and it means the children feel they have participated when the baby is placed in the manger on Christmas Day.

During recent years, thanks to the Church of England Children's Society, Christingle services have become very popular during the Advent and Christmas seasons. The Christingle comes originally from Moravia. It is made by wrapping a red ribbon round an orange, placing a candle with a sheath of aluminium foil in the top, and sticking four cocktail sticks of fruit and nuts around the candle into the top of the orange.

The orange symbolizes the world.
The candle symbolizes Jesus, the light of the world.
The ribbon symbolizes the blood of Jesus.
The four sticks symbolize the four seasons.
The fruit symbolizes the fruits of the earth.
The whole shows God's love for his world and for each of us.

[1] From Stocking Fillas Ltd, Tennant House, London Road, Macclesfield, Cheshire SL11 0W.
[2] Gertrud Mueller Nelson, *op. cit.* p.67.

If your church holds such a service then the christingle can be taken home to provide the centre-piece for a special meal. If not a Christingle tea party could be a means of sharing the love of God at Christmas with both Christian and non-Christian friends. The last Sunday in Advent or the first after Christmas would be ideal occasions.

3. Epiphany

With all the excitement of Christmas, Epiphany very easily gets lost, but a little celebration makes the removal of the Christmas decorations much easier for the children. The French have a tradition for celebrating with a special cake, a gateau des rois. These are usually made of puff pastry and marzipan with a dried bean placed inside. The one who gets the bean becomes the king and wears the crown for the rest of the meal. Owing to the fact that our children like neither pastry nor marzipan I simply make a favourite cake, decorated with a large star and stand the three kings from the crib scene with it on the table. Last Christmas we had three real kings, the two-year-old, four-year-old and a visiting three-year-old. All wore elaborate crowns that had been made earlier in the day and we played 'Hunt the Star', an adapted version of hunt the thimble, using a cardboard star instead. Older children may, with a little help, enjoy making up a simple board game using counters (or buttons) and dice.[1] Constructing it would make a happy post-Christmas family activity. The idea of a desert journey can provide the instructions—sandstorms, lame camels, an oasis, sighting the star, losing the map, meeting friendly nomads can all be the reasons for moving forwards or backwards with the aim being to arrive finally at the stable.

4. Lent

Lent is traditionally a time of abstinence, a time for giving up things like chocolate or alcohol. Useful though exercises in abstinence may be, Lent is also an opportunity for positive Christian teaching as well; a period of time long enough to achieve some specific goal and yet short enough to make some special devotional effort which doesn't seem possible all the year round. It is a time, like Advent, when families may be able to undertake family together prayers, perhaps some of the Easter story could be learned by heart as a corporate activity. Parents could consider using this time as an opportunity to get up early to pray, or to make a special effort to use an evening during the week to read a Lent book.

Lent, perhaps more than the other seasons of the Christian Year, is a time which can 'grow' with the age of the children. Very small children may enjoy pancakes on Shrove Tuesday, but are unlikely to understand much more of the season before Holy Week. Once the oldest child is about five years, a simple time of penitence can be appropriate for Ash Wednesday. We have friends with four children, ranging from 10 to 3, who have devised an activity which each family member can join in. After the evening meal each person is given a pencil and a piece of paper and they then write or draw something for which they would like to say sorry. The youngest obviously needs some help. The papers are then folded and placed in a roasting tin in the middle of the table and burnt. They then use the ash to mark each others' foreheads with a cross. For small children Teddy Horsley's *The Grumpy Day* may help.[2]

[1] See Gertrud Mueller Nelson *op. cit.* p.122.
[2] Leslie Francis and Nicola Slee *The Grumpy Day* (British and Foreign Bible Society, Swindon, 1989).

In an attempt to make something special for each day of Lent which would be suitable for a mixed age range of children, a friend and I got together to devise a Lenten calendar. We came up with two ideas based on Biblical images of God and his promises, each having a symbol to represent it. Our list is on page 24 below, but there are many others which could equally well have been used.

Lenten Tree of Life
A large sheet of paper is put up on the wall with a leafless tree on it. Each day one child chooses a symbol and draws it on a 'leaf' of paper and sticks it on the tree. By Easter the tree is bursting with life-giving leaves.

Lenten Journey
This again requires a large sheet of paper on the wall with a pathway leading to a tomb. There needs to be a square for each day of Lent.

With very small children this would ideally be prepared beforehand with a symbol drawn on each square and another square of plain paper, perhaps with the date on, stuck over with blutak. Each day the top square can be removed, providing an opportunity to talk about the meaning of each symbol. As children grow older they can prepare the calendar themselves. The tomb can have a removable 'stone' and the completed journey can be decorated according to the abilities and ages of the children.

Over a period of years, most, if not all, of these promises will be learnt by the participating children—it's worth including the reference on the leaf or square. These could be adapted to make alternative Advent calendars and Old Testament prophecies of the coming Messiah could be used for the leaves or stepping stones to the stable.

A Lent Corner
Even quite young children can enjoy and use a special place for Lent—some pictures of deserts, a bowl of sand, a cactus, a small collection of books. This could be a focus place for family together prayers or simply for bedtime prayers during this time.

5. Maundy Thursday
The events of the last few days of Jesus' life are not easy for many small children to cope with. For years we have had to adapt the endings of a number of traditional fairy tales. In our house the gingerbread man hops off the fox's nose onto the river bank, the little pigs all live happily in the house of bricks, and so on. If this is needed for storybook characters, whatever do we do with the real events of the crucifixion? Carefully selected books together with several family activities have provided a way forward.

We have no Jewish connections and have made no attempt to turn Maundy Thursday supper into Passover, but we do try to use it as a way of acting out the events of the Last Supper. A family meal of roast lamb, matzos, red wine for the adults and ribena for the children provides the setting for us to read the account of Jesus' last supper with his disciples and his

subsequent betrayal. We wash each other's feet and talk about serving one another and pray 'Thank you' prayers for all that Jesus has done for us and all that he has taught us. As the children grow older they can participate more and a simple table liturgy may be appropriate. Perhaps offers of service could be exchanged:
—an older child might offer to wash the car, clean the shoes, help a younger sibling.
—a parent might offer to do a chore normally undertaken by the child or help to do something the child finds difficult alone.
—a younger child might be encouraged to lay the table or make a picture especially for someone else.

6. Good Friday
After church on Good Friday can be an excellent time to make an Easter garden. The first time we tried this Sarah was only two and we were living in Muscat. Soil and flowers were out of the question, but a trip to the beach provided us with stones to make a tomb, sand and shells for decoration. I will never forget the wonder in her voice when she looked into the 'tomb' at crack of dawn on Easter morning and said 'It's empty!'. More traditionally an Easter garden is made by filling a container with earth; a roasting tin lined with tin foil works well. This provides sufficient depth to plant daisies or primulas. Carrot tops which have sprouted in water look effective if they have been started about two weeks earlier. Crosses can be made by binding twigs together with thread or fine string and the cave tomb by balancing some larger stones. As the children place the crosses in the earth and put a stone in front of the tomb, so the account of the first Good Friday is recounted for them. There is no doubt that even such a simple activity as this can be a vehicle of learning religious truth and a cause for awe and excitement. I don't know why, having made the garden with her brother and father, my daughter doesn't automatically assume that the stone is rolled away by her parents after she has gone to bed on Saturday night. But to her the rolled back stone is evidence of an angel and her amazement on Easter morning in turn renews a sense of resurrection wonder in her parents.

7. Easter Day
An Easter Tree
Eggs as symbols of new life have long been associated with Easter and painting eggshells is a fun activity for even very young children. Blowing eggs is not difficult as long as a good sized pin is poked into both ends. Once the yolk is burst, the contents can be blown into a bowl, then the shells rinsed out and decorated in whatever manner the child chooses.

One very effective way is to use a mixture of wax and coloured dyes.
1. First, put blown eggs into a light dye, e.g. yellow.
2. Using a match and a candle, drip wax onto the egg to make a pattern.
3. Put into a stronger dye—red/blue/green.
4. Repeat this process of wax and dye 3 or 4 times.
5. Place eggs on kitchen paper in a warm oven to remove wax.

Faces are fun to paint on eggs and as children grow older so their patterns can become increasingly complex. For young children it is simpler to use cracked egg shells rather than blown ones. I just save all the broken egg shells used during Holy Week, rinse them out and save them for decorating on Easter Eve. Half shells are easier for small hands to hold without smudging the painting they have already done, and they are much easier to hang up. An Easter tree makes a most attractive and simple decoration. Any branch or twig can be used and placed in a flowerpot full of earth. A reasonably sized pot plant would work just as well.

First the shells need to be decorated. They can be dyed using food colouring or the special dyes which are available in some art shops and stationers. A pack of 6 dyes is available for about 60p. Felt-tip pens are also effective for patterns and faces. We used a small set of pearlized paints from the Early Learning Centre, and dabbed the different colours on using a tissue. To hang the painted shells up you need a needle, some thread and a few beads. Take a length of thread and tie a bead (or small button) in the middle. Thread the two loose ends through a needle and pass it through the eggshell from the underside. Remove the needle, then tie the ends and the shell is ready for hanging.

Easter Breakfast
Early morning is a special time at Easter. Why not get up with your early risers and have a party? Easter breakfast can be made special without a great deal of effort. Hot Cross buns and croissants are delicious and readily available. Children who like hard-boiled eggs will love eating coloured ones dyed the previous day. Cold ham and cheese are good on toast and can make a change from marmalade or marmite. Each of our children has a decorated coloured egg which is kept from year to year and this is filled the night before and hidden very early on Easter morning. In order to avoid too much chocolate I try to find something small to go inside which they can wear new to church—a pair of socks or tights, a belt or gloves. A new face flannel or a bar of soap would also make suitable egg fillers. Anything indeed which can in an inexpensive way emphasize the truth that Easter is a time for new beginnings.

One family we know uses Easter breakfast as an opportunity to give each member a new book—something which will help them learn something more about God. When I was single Easter breakfast was a meal I enjoyed sharing with others. It does become more difficult if guests are being invited to lunch, but perhaps two families could plan together, breakfast at one house and lunch at the other, single friends can be invited and the pressure to clear up before church as well as organize lunch is avoided.

8. Pentecost
Pentecost is a festival which brings with it a host of different symbols. It is a Jewish festival which marks the birthday of the church, and as such offers a variety of activities which would be appropriate. When the Holy Spirit first came to the disciples Pentecost was being celebrated by the Jews. Pentecost (*Pentekosta* in Greek, meaning fifty) fell fifty days after the Passover. It was a spring festival celebrating the wheat harvest and also commemorated the giving of the Law to Moses on Mount Sinai.

Jan Wilson provides several recipes of Jewish origin in *Feasting for Festivals.*[1] Wind, fire, the fruit and gifts of the Spirit are all aspects of Pentecost which can provide the basis for games or craft ideas which could help a family to celebrate. Kites, balloons and windmills can all be used to help illustrate the fact that although we cannot see the Spirit (wind) we can see his effects. A mobile is also a fun and appropriate activity. Gertrud Mueller Nelson[2] suggests a red cardboard dove surrounded by seven orange flames to mark the gifts of the Spirit.

I have a friend whose children seemed to be constantly at each other's throats. She devised a sticker chart for each family member for a week. The idea was that at the end of each day each person awarded a fruit (of the Spirit) to someone else. A child might award patience to Mum or kindness to a sibling and so on. The family was both on the look-out for good fruit in others and keen to be exhibiting it themselves. This would be both a practical and a fun way to learn the fruits of the Spirit during a period of the following Pentecost.

Each year each family will provide its own opportunities for celebration and learning. Birthdays, wedding anniversaries, baptisms (and their anniversaries), new homes, new school years, can all, with a little imagination, be turned into occasions, opportunities to celebrate and to have 'God conversations' with our children. It is my hope and prayer that some of the ideas in this booklet might spur you on to think of your own, and that you might share them with your friends.

[1] Jan Wilson, *op. cit.* pp.62-64.
[2] Gertrud Mueller Nelson, *op. cit.* p.192.

APPENDIX

Suggestions for Promises of God with symbols and Bible references which could be used during Lent (see page 20):

Promises	Symbol	Reference
OF SALVATION	the Cross	Col 1.19,20
	lamb	John 1.29
	fish (icthus)	Jesus Christ, Son of God, Saviour
	rainbow	Genesis 9.13
	washing powder	Isaiah 1.18
TO GIVE LIGHT	candle	John 8.12
	sun	Genesis 1.3
	moon	Genesis 1.5
TO GUIDE	feet	Psalm 18.33
	door	John 10.7
	signpost	John 14.6
TO SAVE	shepherd's crook	Psalm 23.1/John 10.14
	arms	Deut. 33.27
	hen & chicks	Luke 13.34
	a heart (symbol of friendship)	John 15.14
	doctor's bag (symbol of healing)	Jeremiah 33.6
	river	Jeremiah 31.9b
	mountains	Psalm 121.1,2
	Holy Spirit H.S.	John 14.26
TO PROVIDE FOR PHYSICAL NEEDS	bread	John 6.35
	wine	Matthew 26.27,28
	water	John 4.14
	bird (sparrow)	Matthew 10.29
	lily	Luke 12.27
TO TEACH	blackboard	Psalm 119.171
	ear	Isaiah 30.21
	vine	John 15.1
	Bible	Psalm 119.89
OF PEACE	olive branch	Genesis 8.11
	dove	John 1.32
OF THE KINGDOM	trumpets	1 Cor. 15.52
	someone singing	Isaiah 12.5
	praying hands	Matthew 6.6
	church	Matthew 16.18
	treasure	Matthew 13.45,46
	fishing nets	Matthew 13.47,48
PICTURES OF GOD	crown/king	Malachi 1.14b
	rock	Psalm 18.2
	alpha/beginning	Rev. 21.6
	omega/end	Rev 22.13
	manger/Emmanuel	Matthew 1.23
	fire	Hebrews 12.29
	Father	Matthew 6.9
	ring/bridegroom	Rev. 18.23
	scales/justice	Ezekiel 20.36
	towel/servant	Luke 22.7